Dream It, Do It!

GET DRAWING!

Charlotte Guillain

raintree

Raintree is an imprint of Capstone Global Library Limited, a company incorporated in England and Wales having its registered office at 7 Pilgrim Street, London, EC4V 6LB – Registered company number: 6695582

www.raintreepublishers.co.uk
myorders@raintreepublishers.co.uk

Text © Capstone Global Library Limited 2014
First published in hardback in 2014
The moral rights of the proprietor have been asserted.

Edited by Rebecca Rissman, Dan Nunn, and Helen Cox Cannons
Designed by Steve Mead
Original illustrations © Capstone Global Library 2014
Picture research by Ruth Blair
Production by Vicki Fitzgerald
Originated by Capstone Global Library Ltd
Printed and bound in China by CTPS

ISBN 978 1 406 27260 4 (hardback)
18 17 16 15 14
10 9 8 7 6 5 4 3 2 1

ISBN 978 1 406 27265 9 (paperback)
19 18 17 16 15 14
10 9 8 7 6 5 4 3 2 1

British Library Cataloguing in Publication Data
A full catalogue record for this book is available from the British Library.

Acknowledgements

We would like to thank the following for permission to reproduce photographs: Alamy pp. 13 (© Anthony Hatley), 21 (© Photo Art Collection (PAC)); Capstone Publishers pp. 15 top & bottom, 16, 17, 26, 27, 28, 29 (all © Karon Dubke), 19 (Steve Walker/Dawn Beacon/Stella Plage); Getty Images pp. 9 (Jupiterimages), 24 (Fotos International), 25 (Trish Gant); iStockphoto p. 23 (© Gabor Izso); Shutterstock pp. 5 (© Artush), 7 left (© ETIENjones), 7 right (© oksana2010), 11 (© sevenke), 12 (© Tenki), 19. Incidental photographs reproduced with permission of: graph paper, Shutterstock (© optimarc); felt tip pens, Shutterstock (© nikkytok); watercolour paper, Shutterstock (© Aleksandr Stennikov). Cover photograph of children drawing into the air reproduced with permission of Getty Images (MECKY).

We would like to thank Adam Guillain for his invaluable help in the preparation of this book.

CONTENTS

Some words are shown in bold, **like this**. You can find out what they mean by looking in the glossary.

BE AN ARTIST!

Have you always wanted to be an artist? Have you dreamed of drawing brilliant pictures but don't know where to start? This book will help you to make your dreams come true.

Read on and find out how to stop dreaming and get drawing!

WHAT DO YOU NEED?

Gather together any of these **materials** you might need to get drawing:

Drawing pencils
Colouring pencils
Drawing pens
Chalk
Charcoal
White and coloured paper
Textured paper
Squared paper
Scrapbook
Sketchbook

Collect all the things you need in one place and try to use something new each time you draw.

FINDING INSPIRATION

Ideas come when you don't expect them. Carry a sketchpad with you and keep all your drawings and doodles. You could also cut out any pictures you like in magazines and stick them in your sketchpad.

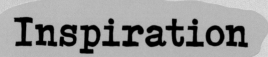 

Inspiration

Decorate the cover of your sketchpad with photos and pictures that inspire you.

PLAYING WITH PENCIL AND PAPER

It's a good idea to warm up when you start drawing. Try taking a line for a walk on a piece of paper and see where it takes you! Practise drawing circles and see how perfect you can make them, or see what they turn into.

Activity

Draw a squiggle for a friend and then get them to finish the squiggle to make a complete drawing. Then swap!

SHAPES

Look for the big shapes in the objects you try to draw. Sketch these shapes lightly first and then start to fill in the details.

Activity

Look carefully in a mirror and see what shapes make up your face. Try to draw a **self-portrait**, starting with the shape of your head and then looking at where your eyes, nose, and mouth sit.

LIGHT AND SHADOW

Light is very important when you're drawing. Experiment by shining a light from different sides and angles on an object you want to draw. How do the shapes and shadows you can see change?

Activity

Try using lines and dots to fill in your drawings. Cross the lines or draw the dots closer together in the dark parts and space them out more in the lighter areas.

DRAWING PEOPLE

Look at people around you and in pictures. How do the different parts of their bodies fit together? How far down their body do their arms reach? What do they look like from the side? Look at how other artists have drawn people.

Activity

1. Stick a sheet of coloured paper on the wall.
2. Get a friend to stand next to the paper and get someone else to shine a torch towards him or her.
3. Draw around the shadow of your friend's head on the piece of paper, then cut it out.
4. You now have a **silhouette** of your friend's head!

ILLUSTRATING STORIES

If you are stuck for ideas of what to draw, try drawing **illustrations** for your favourite books. Think about the characters before you start – how will you show their personalities? If the book already has pictures, try to choose a section that doesn't have illustrations.

Inspiration

Look at other illustrators' drawings. Whose style do you like? Try copying their drawings and develop your own style using theirs as a starting point.

GET COLOURFUL

You can enjoy experimenting with colour when you draw. Look carefully at the colours of things that you draw. How do they change in light and shadow? You can use unusual colours to show different feelings and moods.

Activity

Draw a picture of yourself looking happy and a picture where you look sad or angry. Which colours could you use to show your different feelings?

What do the colours in this painting tell you about how the girl is feeling?

LOOK DIFFERENTLY

When you're drawing, it is interesting to look at the world around you in new and different ways. Try drawing things from different viewpoints, for example, looking down from above or up from below. Or you could try drawing things upside down!

Activity

Choose one section of the thing you want to draw. Zoom in so you draw that part **magnified** very close up.

DRAWING CARTOONS

Do you like reading comics or watching cartoons? Try drawing your own cartoons. Look at how the **illustrations** in comics show people and objects in a different way to other artists. Practise copying their styles and then make your own comic strip telling a short story or joke.

Activity

In a small notebook, draw a cartoon character on the first page. On each page that follows, draw the same character but move him or her slightly each time. When you've finished, flick the pages of the book and watch your character move!

SET UP A GALLERY

All artists need to share their work! Put your drawings in a gallery.

1. Choose your best drawings. Don't show too many – just choose the pictures you are especially proud of. Try to show a range of pictures that use pencil, pen, crayon, chalk, and different types of paper. Can you show drawings in different styles?

2. You want your drawings to look good hanging on the wall. **Mount** each picture by sticking it onto coloured card that is slightly larger.

3. Write some information about each picture. How did you get the idea to draw it and what materials did you use? Stick this information onto the corner of each mount.

4. Either stick your drawings on a blank wall or lay them out onto a table.

5. Make a **catalogue** for the people who are going to visit your gallery. This could be a leaflet with some information about you and how you got into drawing. Then list all the drawings that you're displaying in your gallery.

6. Invite your friends and family to a **private view**. Offer them a drink and some snacks and talk to them about your drawings. They might have lots of questions for you!

7. Make sure you take lots of photos of your gallery for your scrapbook.

8. Start thinking of ideas for your next drawings!

GLOSSARY

catalogue complete list of items

charcoal stick of burned wood or other matter used for drawing

illustration drawing or painting that shows events or characters in a story

magnified something that has been made to look larger than it really is

materials things needed for an activity

mount fix into position to display

private view special viewing of art in a gallery to which people are invited

self-portrait picture of yourself

silhouette outline of something dark against a light background

textured having a surface that has a pattern or bumps on it

FIND OUT MORE

Books

Drawing is Cool: Learn How to Draw Everything! (Arcturus Publishing Ltd, 2011)

Illustration School: Let's Draw Happy People, Sachiko Umoto (Quarry, 2010)

Websites

www.activityvillage.co.uk/learn_to_draw.htm
This website has printable step-by-step worksheets to help you learn to draw.

www.guardian.co.uk/childrens-books-site/series/how-to-draw
Children's book illustrators show you how to draw.

INDEX